SPOTLIGHT ON
CIVIC COURAGE
HEROES OF CONSCIENCE™

HARVEY MILK

THE FIRST OPENLY GAY ELECTED OFFICIAL IN THE UNITED STATES

Barbara Gottfried Hollander

New York

This book is dedicated to Cynthia Ruth Holt—your friendship and ability to be there for others is unparalleled. Like your relative Susan B. Anthony, you fight for what you believe in, making a difference in many people's lives. The world is a better place because of you.

Published in 2018 by The Rosen Publishing Group, Inc.
29 East 21st Street, New York, NY 10010

Library of Congress Cataloging-in-Publication Data

Names: Hollander, Barbara Gottfried, 1970– author.
Title: Harvey Milk: the first openly gay elected official in the United States / Barbara Gottfried Hollander.
Other titles: First openly gay elected official in the United States
Description: New York : Rosen YA, [2018] | Series: Spotlight on civic courage: heroes of conscience | Includes bibliographical references and index. | Audience: Grades 5–10.
Identifiers: LCCN 2017012600| ISBN 9781538380956 (library bound) | ISBN 9781538380925 (pbk.) | ISBN 9781538380932 (6 pack)
Subjects: LCSH: Milk, Harvey—Juvenile literature. | Politicians—California—San Francisco—Biography—Juvenile literature. | Gay politicians—California—San Francisco—Biography—Juvenile literature. | San Francisco (Calif.)—Politics and government—20th century—Juvenile literature. | San Francisco (Calif)—Biography—Juvenile literature. | Gay liberation movement—California—San Francisco—History—20th century—Juvenile literature.
Classification: LCC F869.S353 M5455 2018 | DDC 324.2092 [B] —dc23
LC record available at https://lccn.loc.gov/2017012600

Manufactured in the United States of America

On the cover: This photo of Harvey Milk was taken in 1977. The background photo, dated November 27, 1979, shows a parade honoring the memory of Milk and Mayor George Moscone on the day of their assassinations.

CONTENTS

Hope Will Never Be Silent 4

Introducing the Milks 6

Being Young Harvey 8

Discovering His Sexuality 10

Going to College 14

Desiring Honorable Discharge.................. 16

Finding Romance.............................. 18

Writing Love Letters............................ 20

Keeping the Secret 22

Becoming Harvey............................ 24

Struggling with Double Identity 26

Moving to Castro Street 28

What's Happening in America?.................. 30

Becoming Political............................ 32

Living on the Political Edge 36

Assassinating the Mayors 38

Creating Prideful Hope 40

Glossary 42

For More Information....................... 43

For Further Reading......................... 45

Bibliography 46

Index 47

HOPE WILL NEVER BE SILENT

Harvey Milk is as synonymous with gay rights as the rainbow flag he commissioned Gilbert Baker to create for the 1978 Gay Pride Parade in San Francisco. On November 8, 1977, Milk became America's first openly gay elected official. Upon achieving a political victory, Milk stated, "This is not my victory, it's yours. If a gay man can win, it proves there is hope for all minorities who are willing to fight." Milk's life was about finding the courage to fight and realizing that "rights are won only by those who make their voices heard." He spent five and a half of his forty-eight years in politics—and only one year in office—before his life was cut short. But Milk's hope—bursting down the closet doors—continues to inspire the actions of his supporters, who take notice of his words: "Hope will never be silent."

Harvey Milk, a leader in the gay rights movement, sits in his camera store on San Francisco's Castro Street. He was assassinated about one-and-a-half years after this photograph was taken.

Introducing the Milks

Harvey Bernard Milk was born on May 22, 1930, in Woodmere, New York, on Long Island, to a Jewish family. His parents were William ("Bill") and Minerva ("Minnie") Karns Milk. Harvey had one older brother, Robert. Their cousin, Helen Milk Mendales, remembers, "[Harvey] was a wild little kid—he and his older brother, Robert. When Robert was probably about 6 years old and his brother was 3 years old … [they] got together … and took all the labels off the cans [of goods]. When my aunt needed a can, it was always a surprise."

Harvey's grandfather Morris, a Lithuanian immigrant, cofounded the Sons of Israel Synagogue (the first synagogue in Woodmere). He also owned a department store called Milks. Harvey's dad worked at the store before heading out West and later enlisting. Both of Harvey's parents served in the Navy during World War I. A Brooklyn-born feminist, Minerva Milk was part of the Yeomanettes, a group that fought for the inclusion of women in the US Navy.

HARVEY

Milk was born on May 22, 1930. Decades life is still celebrated at festivities in San co during Pride Month.

MAY 22, 2016

Being Young Harvey

When he was younger, Harvey Milk's nickname was Glimpy Milch. The name Glimpy referred to his physical appearance because he had "flappy ears and oversized feet that early on made him look like a character from a Walt Disney cartoon." His grandfather Morris's given surname was Milch before immigrating to the United States. As a young boy, Harvey went to Lone Ranger matinée movies with Robert. Harvey's favorite part was the matinée raffle because the winner had a moment in the spotlight. Harvey also liked opera, attending performances at the old Metropolitan Opera House in New York City. Harvey's favorite composers included Mahler, Strauss, and Wagner. (He said his tastes were too sophisticated for Verdi.) Harvey wore the number 60 jersey as a linebacker for the Bay Shore High School football team. He also worked for his father's business, Bay Shore Furriers.

Young Harvey loved matinées featuring the Lone Ranger. This fifteen-part serial was about a masked ranger and his Native American friend, Tonto, fighting outlaws in the Old West.

DISCOVERING HIS SEXUALITY

Harvey knew he was gay in high school but did not express his sexual orientation at home or in school. His mother, Minnie, often warned her son to stay away from homosexuals, suggesting that they did bad things to others. Harvey "would protect Minnie, he decided, by keeping it [being gay] a secret." Likewise at school, Harvey hid his sexuality. He feared being beaten up in the locker room or made the brunt of jokes. Harvey was even careful with what he shared with classmates, worried that certain interests would make people question his sexuality. One of his sports friends, Dick Brown, remarked, "He kept his secret well ...The one thing that gets me mad is here I'm supposed

to be one of his good buddies, but he never trusted me enough to tell. I can't say how I would have reacted. I guess I would have ostracized him."

Harvey Milk attended Bay Shore High School on Long Island. He hid the fact that he was gay at school, but he would meet other gay men in New York City and on Fire Island.

This photo of Central Park was taken on a night in 1947. Here in this Manhattan park, Milk did not have to hide his sexuality.

In his youth, Harvey found places where he could be more open about his sexuality, like Central Park and the standing room only area at the Met, but these New York locations carried risk. The police in Central Park routinely rounded up homosexuals. Officers cited them for indecent exposure because some gay men were shirtless. (Some straight men were shirtless, too, but they were left alone.) "Anger had no place among homosexuals of those years, only fear," writes Randy Shilts in *The Mayor of Castro Street.* "Not only fear of the police, but fear of himself and his [Harvey's] secret being revealed by an afternoon's routine police action." In August 1947, police arrested a shirtless Harvey, then seventeen, but they did not book him. A classmate of Harvey's shared in Shilts's book, "[Harvey] … had to face [how badly people viewed homosexuals] all by himself. It really is terrible to think about. It must have been traumatic for him."

GOING TO COLLEGE

Milk encountered both religious and sexual discrimination in his life. He also saw his family create opportunities to confront discrimination. Milk's grandfather Morris began a Jewish hunt club in Woodmere when the local club would not admit Jews. At Milk's college, the New York State College for Teachers at Albany (now known as University at Albany, State University of New York) most fraternities did not admit Jews either—so Milk joined a Jewish fraternity, Kappa Beta, and advocated for its inclusion of all religions. Milk pursued a degree in education, focusing on history and math. He wrote a newspaper column exploring the issue of diversity. Later, Milk became the *State College News* sports editor, traveling with the basketball team—but resigned in his senior year. Milk spent weekends off campus, not sharing his whereabouts with classmates. He continued his pattern from childhood—having many friends, but none very close to him, and leading a double life.

Harvey Milk, pictured in his 1951 college yearbook, wrote a weekly column in his college newspaper, which included lessons learned from the atrocities of World War II (1939–1945).

DESIRING HONORABLE DISCHARGE

In June 1951, just three months after his college graduation, Milk enlisted in the Navy. He rose up the ranks quickly, serving as communications officer, lieutenant junior grade, and chief petty officer of the submarine rescue ship, *Kittiwake.* Milk was the coach of his ship's wrestling team. He was also a deep-sea diving officer and later an instructor. Milk served in the Navy for almost four years, including during the Korean War. During this time, Milk continued to keep his sexuality a secret. Milk and his gay friends spent time together off base at his San Diego apartment on weekend passes and were often joined by other gay men. In 1955, Milk resigned from the Navy officer when he was asked about his sexual orientation. Har-

Harvey Milk's nephew, Stuart Milk (*center*), attended a ship-naming ceremony for the *Harvey Milk* in 2016. The US Navy named six ships after human and civic rights leaders.

vey knew of many men dishonorably discharged from the US Navy for being gay. He did not want to face this kind of discrimination.

Finding Romance

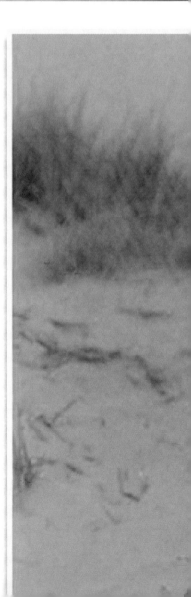

I n June 1956, twenty-six-year-old Milk met nineteen-year-old Joe Campbell at Riis Park Beach in Queens, New York. Campbell longed to be cared for, and Milk wanted to care for someone. Campbell moved into Milk's Rego Park apartment a few weeks later, although Milk continued to hide his sexual orientation from his family. During the day, Milk taught math and history at Long Island's Hewlitt High School, while Campbell decorated furniture. One day, Milk and Campbell packed up and drove their Plymouth Savoy to Texas because Milk wanted to live in warmer weather. After Milk encountered religious discrimination in his workplace, they returned to New York, and Milk worked as an actuary. Milk and Campbell's relationship lasted six years—the longest union Milk would ever have. Campbell will forever be remembered as the "Sugar Plum Fairy" in the song "Walk on the Wild Side" by Lou Reed.

Meeting Joe Campbell changed Harvey Milk's life. Their union, which lasted from 1956 to 1962, was the longest relationship either man would ever have.

WRITING LOVE LETTERS

During their relationship, Milk courted Campbell with romantic poems, gifts, and love letters written from New York, Miami Beach, and Puerto Rico. In his letters, Milk referred to Campbell as Joesan and himself as Harveysan. For their second anniversary, Milk wrote, "the first two [years] have swept by and with each I have found I love you 365 days more." In his March 8, 1963, letter from Puerto Rico, Milk penned, "I miss you very much & hope you realize how much I do love you." Despite these declarations of enduring love, the couple eventually broke up. Although he initiated the breakup, Milk wanted to reconcile soon after Campbell moved from their apartment on Ninety-Sixth Street and Central Park West. Milk even wrote Campbell a pleading note asking him to come back, but Campbell did not return. He believed Milk would eventually find someone else.

Dear Joeson

I don't want to write this but I can not help myself for I have been feeling very strange lately & the pain is indeed deep — So I have to tell you that I love you so much & miss you so much that I have tears as I write this. I wish me pray that you will call & say that you want me — but I tell myself not to think this for you have told me that you do not want me anylonger — Nevertheless I do so love you & I am so lonesome for you that I do not even want to stay home for more than I have to as I see you whenever I am in the apartment. — I'm so sorry that we are not together & wish so much to

[caption overlapping letter:]

The collection at the San Francisco Public Library houses many love letters exchanged between Harvey Milk and Joe Campbell. Milk's letters convey his strong feelings for his first love.

hol ... forgive me for
wi ... o feel
like I am ... in heart —
I miss you — I love you — I want you —

as always

KEEPING THE SECRET

Campbell was right. In 1962, thirty-three-year-old Milk began dating Craig Rodwell, who was ten years his junior. One year later, Milk landed a job at the Wall Street firm Bache and Company, first as a researcher and later as a supervisor. Milk opened Rodwell's eyes to the world of opera, museums, and fine dining. Rodwell exposed Milk to something he was not ready for—being publicly gay. Rodwell once remarked that Milk had everything, "but the chance to be openly who you are, like a normal human being." Milk displayed conservative leanings both at work and in politics. But Rodwell leaned left and participated in gay civil rights events, like the Stone-

wall Riots. Milk wanted to keep his life compartmentalized, so Milk and Rodwell eventually broke up. Milk then dated other men, but sixteen-year-old Jack Galen McKinley changed his life. This young man made Milk question the need for a double life.

Tired of being targeted by the police, customers and supporters of the gay club the Stonewall Inn began rioting on June 28, 1969. Demonstrations in New York continued days later.

BECOMING HARVEY

McKinley moved into Milk's New York apartment shortly after they met. About four years later, in 1967, they moved to Texas, but before long they returned to New York.

Milk and McKinley had a rocky relationship. Together, they dealt with McKinley's substance addictions and his mental health challenges, including battling depression and attempted suicides. Their relationship had a profound effect on Milk, who quit his Wall Street job and became increasingly more liberal and open. When they first met, Milk acted as McKinley's protector. But years later, when McKinley landed a stage manager job in the San Francisco production of *Hair*, it was Milk who followed McKinley to California. The move was a turning point—a chance for Milk to stop leading a double life. After McKinley and Milk broke up, McKinley moved back to New York to work for director Tom O'Horgan, but Milk stayed in California.

Milk, shown here in 1978, followed McKinley to San Francisco, California. McKinley worked as a stage manager in *Hair*, and Milk found a job in finance.

STRUGGLING WITH DOUBLE IDENTITY

Upon his initial move to California, Milk continued to lead a double life. At work, he was "Conservative Harvey," catering to the big business establishment. At home, he was "Liberal Harvey," where he was open about his sexual identity and increasingly more liberal in his political views. An event on April 29, 1970—the US invasion of Cambodia—prompted these two Milks to clash. One day, Milk joined an anti-invasion protest, publicly speaking out against big business. He even set his BankAmericard on fire.

Milk's appearance had also changed. The clean-shaven Milk had given way to a long-haired man, often referenced as "Harvey the Hippie." When Milk's firm demanded a haircut, Milk refused and was fired.

Milk then enjoyed a brief stint in New York again, and on his forty-first birthday met Joseph Scott Smith. The two met while working together on O'Horgan's play *Inner City*—along with Milk's former boyfriend McKinley.

Sean Penn won an Oscar for his portrayal of Harvey Milk in the 2008 biopic, *Milk*. This film depicts the life of Harvey Milk and his fight for the rights of the gay community.

MOVING TO CASTRO STREET

Milk began a new phase of his life with this new partner. Smith was twenty years younger than Milk, with blond hair and blue eyes. Eventually, the couple moved to California, got a dog named The Kid, and spent almost an entire year traveling the state in a green Dodge Charger. At the end of 1972, they settled on San Francisco's Castro Street—a mainly Irish neighborhood with two gay bars. In 1973, Milk and Smith opened Castro Camera, with a sign that read, "Yes, We Are Very Open." The store featured a large maroon couch, next to a barber chair that often held The Kid. On some days, Smith tended store while Milk chatted with local merchants, creating bridges between the newer gay shop owners and straight old-timers. On other days, Milk sat on his shop's couch helping people with issues from battling alcoholism to finding a job.

In the film *Milk* (2008), James Franco portrayed Scott Smith. After the end of their relationship, Milk and Smith remained friends and business partners.

WHAT'S HAPPENING IN AMERICA?

In the time leading up to Milk and Smith's move to 577 Castro Street, Apartment 304, persecution of gays in San Francisco—and throughout the United States—was rampant. But the stage was slowly being set for change. Gays faced employment discrimination, arrests, purging from military and government positions, police raids, and business closings. Gay bars were a particular target. According to Randy Shilts's book, from 1963 to 1964, twelve out of thirty San Francisco gay bars were closed by the police—prompting the formation of the Society for Individual Rights (SIR). By 1967, SIR was the largest gay group, with 1,200 members. Yet, the persecution of gays in the United States continued. By 1971, an average of 2,800 gay people were arrested annually because of their sexual orientation. Some verdicts carried punishments more severe than those for rape or murder. Milk would respond, "Wake up America … No more racism, no more sexism, no more ageism, no more hatred."

San Francisco became a haven for the gay community—particularly the Castro District—named for the landmark Castro Theatre, built in 1922.

BECOMING POLITICAL

Milk did not view the government as representative of everyone and in a campaign speech once stated, "I will strive to bring the government to the people, be they intellectuals or fellow homosexuals, be they blacks or fellow Jews, be they the tax-starved elderly or fellow small shop owners, be they taxi drivers or newspaper reporters." Several events motivated Milk to enter politics. First, to keep Castro Camera open, Milk had to pay a 100-dollar deposit against sales tax. He viewed this practice as preferential treatment for wealthy business owners, who were more likely to have this cash on hand. Secondly, a local

teacher asked Milk to borrow a slide projector that her school could not readily provide. Milk was upset that government funds went to roads and airport expansions that benefited wealthy business owners—but not to schools.

"A gay person in office can set a tone, can command respect … from the young people in our own community who need both examples and hope," said Milk.

The final straw came from former US attorney general John Mitchell's testimony at the Senate's Watergate hearings, which Milk viewed as evidence of government corruption. Milk had a choice: "I am forty-three years old now … I can concentrate on making a lot of money while I enjoy perhaps another ten years of active gay life. Then …

Shown here is Milk's first campaign button from his run for San Francisco Board of Supervisors in 1973. Milk lost that election but kept trying until he won a seat in 1977.

just coast … Or I can get involved and do something about the things that are wrong in this society." Two weeks after Mitchell's testimony, on July 26, 1973, Milk announced his candidacy for San Francisco Board of Supervisors. He lost the election but increased his community involvement. In 1974, when the local merchants' association did not admit gay members, Milk founded the Castro Village Association, admitting both gay and straight members. When Teamster official Allan Baird wanted gay community support for the Coors boycott, Milk agreed, on the condition that Teamsters hire gay drivers, too. From 1974 to 1975, Milk and Smith hosted Castro Street Fairs, partly to register voters, and thousands attended.

Living on the Political Edge

In 1975, Milk ran for Board of Supervisors again and endorsed George Moscone for mayor. Milk lost, but Moscone won. In 1976, Moscone appointed Milk to the Board of Permit Appeals—making Milk the country's first openly gay commissioner. Milk lost two other elections, for both Sixth Congressional District delegate to a national conference and state assemblyman. Finally, Milk won as District 5 supervisor on November 8, 1977. As supervisor, Milk's legislative actions included support of gay rights, environmental protections, and a free public transit program resolution. Milk sponsored a gay rights bill aimed at providing equal rights for gay and straight people. The bill passed with a vote of ten to one; Dan White cast the only vote against it. Later, California senator John Briggs introduced Proposition 6, intending to fire all gay teachers and their supporters. With Milk's help, Proposition 6 was defeated, with about 58 percent of voters voting no.

Harvey Milk and George Moscone both ran for political office in 1975. Moscone won as mayor and gave Milk a job in his administration.

ASSASSINATING THE MAYORS

Milk, the unofficial mayor of Castro Street, received many death threats. He said, "I fully realize that … a gay activist becomes the … potential target for a person who is insecure, terrified, afraid, or very disturbed." During the June 25, 1978, Gay Freedom Day Parade, Milk's manager Anne Kronenberg worried that Milk was a visible target for assassination. On November 27, 1978, her fears came true. Angered by the Proposition 6 failure and the Gay Freedom Day Parade, District 6 city supervisor Dan White resigned. When attempts to get his job back were unsuccessful, White shot Mayor Moscone three times in the chest. Then White went to Milk's office and shot him four times in the chest and once in the head. White was convicted of voluntary manslaughter instead of first-degree murder. The lighter sentence associated with this charge set off the White Night Riots. He was sentenced to seven years in prison, released early, and committed suicide.

A proud Harvey Milk poses in front of his store after winning election and becoming the first openly gay elected official in the United States.

CREATING PRIDEFUL HOPE

Named one of *Time* magazine's most influential people of the twentieth century, Milk created opportunities for equal rights. He inspired change even after his death—like the first National March on Washington for Gay and Lesbian Rights on October 14, 1979, which nationalized the gay rights movement. His legacy continues. There's an annual Harvey Milk Day on May 22, a Harvey Milk High School in New York City, a Harvey Milk Promenade Park and Equality Plaza in Long Beach, California, and a three-act opera called *Harvey Milk*. The film *The Times of Harvey Milk* won a 1985 Oscar, and actor Sean Penn later won a 2009 Oscar for his portrayal of

Milk in another biographical film. Milk even appears on a postage stamp and as the namesake of a US Navy ship. Milk once said people need, "Hope for a better world, hope for a better tomorrow." Milk provided that hope by "stand[ing] for the equal rights for all people."

A bust of Harvey Milk, with his tie blowing in the wind, sits outside his former office—the only bust of a supervisor in San Francisco's City Hall.

GLOSSARY

actuary Someone who puts together and studies statistics for the purpose of figuring out insurance risks and payments.

advocate To support or endorse in a public manner.

assassination The action of suddenly or secretly murdering a person, particularly someone famous.

book To create an official record with a name and personal information, such as a criminal suspect.

corruption Untruthful or false actions, usually by powerful people and often including bribery.

depression Disorder characterized by sadness, hopelessness, apathy, and loss of appetite and sleep.

discrimination Prejudiced actions or perceptions.

dishonorable discharge The termination of a person from the armed forces because of moral or criminal behavior.

endorse To publicly express support.

fraternity A men's society at college or university.

gay Involving sexual desire toward the same sex.

inclusion An act of bringing in as part of a group.

legislative Involving the government branch that makes laws.

ostracize To exclude from a group.

persecute To punish or harass with intent to harm or cause grievance.

preferential Giving priority or favor, special.

purge To suddenly or violently remove a specific group of unwanted people from an organization.

rampant Out of control, usually something disagreeable.

resolution An official demonstration of opinion, such as by a government or other organization.

sexuality An expression of interest involving sex.

sexual orientation A person's sexual identity, such as heterosexual or homosexual. It describes the gender to which one is attracted.

synonymous Closely related to or associated with something.

FOR MORE INFORMATION

American Civil Liberties Union (ACLU)

125 Broad Street, 18th Floor

New York, NY 10004

212-549-2500

Website: https://www.aclu.org/issues/lgbt-rights

Facebook: @aclu.nationwide

Twitter: @ACLU

The ACLU promotes the civil rights of everyone, including lesbian, gay, bisexual, and transgender people. It combats discrimination and seeks to create a world with equal rights for all.

Egale Canada

185 Carlton Street

Toronto, ON M5A 2K7

Canada

(416) 964-7887

Website: http://egale.ca

Facebook: @EgaleCanada

Twitter: @egalecanada

Google+: @EgaleCanada

Instagram: @egalecanada

This organization aims to rid the world of oppression, including homophobia, biphobia, and transphobia. It also provides videos, campaigns, and books to increase understanding and promote opportunities for people of all sexual orientations.

Harvey Milk Foundation (HMF)

PO Box 5666

Fort Lauderdale, FL 33310

(954) 240-8819

Website: http://milkfoundation.org

Facebook: @Harvey.Milk.Foundation

The HMF's efforts promote equality in America and throughout the world. Its site also shares information about Milk's life and his vision for a world without hate.

Human Rights Campaign (HRC)
1640 Rhode Island Avenue NW
Washington, DC 20036
(800) 777-4723
Website: http://www.hrc.org
Facebook: @humanrightscampaign
Twitter: @HRC
Instagram: @humanrightscampaign
Google+: @HRC
Pinterest: @hrcequality
HRC is the largest civil rights organization in the United States. It promotes a world where lesbian, gay, bisexual, and transgender people are equal members of society at home, work, and in communities.

San Francisco Public Library
James C. Hormel LGBTQIA Center—3rd Floor
100 Larkin Street
San Francisco, CA 94102
(415) 557-4400
Website: http://sfpl.org/?pg=0200002401
Among other exhibits, the center features more than fifty letters written from Harvey Milk to Joseph Campbell. Most of these letters were penned after Milk and Campbell's relationship was over.

WEBSITES

Because of the changing nature of internet links, Rosen Publishing has developed an online list of websites related to the subject of this book. This site is updated regularly. Please use this link to access this list:

http://www.rosenlinks.com/CIVC/Milk

FOR FURTHER READING

Aretha, David. *No Compromise: The Story of Harvey Milk*. Greensboro, NC: Morgan Reynold Publishing, 2009.

Black, Dustin Lance, and Armistead Maupin. *Milk: A Pictorial History of Harvey Milk*. New York, NY: Newmarket Press, 2009.

Daley, James. *Great Speeches on Gay Rights*. Mineola, NY: Dover Publications, Inc., 2010.

Downs, Jim. *Stand By Me: The Forgotten History of Gay Liberation*. New York, NY: Basic Books, 2016.

Faderman, Lillian. *The Gay Revolution: The Story of the Struggle*. New York, NY: Simon & Schuster, 2016.

Jones, Cleve. *When We Rise: My Life in the Movement*. New York, NY: Hachette Book Group, 2016.

Milk, Harvey. *An Archive of Hope: Harvey Milk's Speeches and Writings*. Berkeley and Los Angeles, CA: University of California Press, 2013.

Reynolds, Andrew. *The Children of Harvey Milk: How LGBTQ Politicians Changed the World*. New York, NY: Oxford University Press, 2017.

Weiss, Mike. *Double Play: The Hidden Passions Behind the Double Assassination of George Moscone and Harvey Milk*. San Francisco, CA: Vince Emery Productions, 2010.

BIBLIOGRAPHY

Arts Desk. "The Voice of Harvey Milk." PBS: Public Broadcasting Service, December 19, 2008. http://www.pbs.org/newshour/art/the-voice-of-harvey-milk.

Chan, Sewell. "Film Evokes Memories for Milk's Relatives." *New York Times*, February 20, 2009. https://cityroom.blogs.nytimes.com/2009/02/20/film-evokes-memories-for-harvey-milks-relatives/?_r=1.

Encyclopedia of World Biography. "Harvey Milk Biography." Retrieved February 2017. http://www.notablebiographies.com/Ma-Mo/Milk-Harvey.html.

Harvey Milk Foundation. "About." Retrieved February 2017. http://milkfoundation.org/about.

Jones, Natalie. "The Life of Harvey Milk." ACLU: American Civil Liberties Union. Retrieved February 2017. https://www.aclu.org/files/pdfs/lgbt/schoolsandyouth/ramona_milk_presentation.pdf.

Milk, Harvey. *The Harvey Milk Interviews*. San Francisco, CA: Vince Emery Productions, 2012.

Milk, Harvey. "Harvey Milk Letters to Joe Campbell." San Francisco Public Library. Retrieved February 2017. https://sfpl.bibliocommons.com/item/show/2912028093_harvey_milk_letters_to_joe_campbell?active_tab=bib_info.

Moriarty, Francis. "White is Convicted of Voluntary Manslaughter." *Washington Post*, May 22, 1979. https://www.washingtonpost.com/archive/politics/1979/05/22/white-is-convicted-of-voluntary-manslaughter/96862993-7903-4a85-ab69-978c73e3fcb8/?utm_term=.8e7a2acc6113.

Shilts, Randy. *The Mayor of Castro Street: The Life and Times of Harvey Milk*. New York, NY: St. Martin's Press, 2008.

INDEX

B

Baird, Allan, 35
Baker, Gilbert, 4
Briggs, John, 37
Brown, Dick, 10

C

Campbell, Joe, 18–22
Castro Camera, 5, 28–29, 32
Castro Street, 13, 28, 30, 35, 38
Castro Street Fairs, 35
Castro Street Village Association, 35
Coors boycott, 35

D

death threats, 38
discrimination, 17, 30–31

G

Gay Freedom Day Parade, 38
Gay Pride Parade, 4
gay rights bill, 36

H

Harvey Milk (opera), 40
Harvey Milk Day, 40

K

Korean War, 16
Kronenberg, Anne, 38

M

Mayor of Castro Street, The (book), 13

McKinley, Jack Galen, 23–25, 27
Milk, Harvey
    activism, 26–27
    childhood, 6–13
    death, 38
    education, 14–15
    legacy, 40–41
    military service, 16–17
    politics, 32–37
Mitchell, John, 34–35
Moscone, George, 36–38

P

Penn, Sean, 27, 40
Proposition 6, 37–38

R

Rodwell, Craig, 22–23

S

Shilts, Randy, 13, 30
Smith, Joseph Scott, 27–30, 35
Society for Individual Rights, 30
Stonewall Riots, 22

T

Teamsters, 35
Times of Harvey Milk, The (film), 40

W

Watergate, 34
White, Dan, 36, 38
White Night Riots, 38

About the Author

Barbara Gottfried Hollander has authored more than twenty-five books, including *Marriage Rights and Gay Rights: Interpreting the Constitution* (Understanding the United States Constitution) and *Ellen DeGeneres: Television's Funniest Host* (Remarkable LGBTQ Lives).

Photo Credits